MW00795960

PERMISSION TO PROSPER

Gicele Wray-Lindley

Permission To Prosper

For bulk orders or bookings, please visit www.lindleybooks.com or auntiegigispeaks.com

Printed in the United States of America

Lindley Books, 2020

ISBN: 978-1-7353319-0-4

Lindley Books

Chicago, IL

USA

www.lindleybooks.com

DEDICATION

This book is dedicated to my mother Isabel Wray who taught me the importance of prayer, faith, diligence, and wisdom in business. I want to acknowledge and thank God for my amazing family. My sisters Shanida and Naomi kept me focused. My husband Omar prayed with me concerning this project. My father Esteban Wray taught me the principles of diligence and hard work.

This book is also dedicated to the countless business owners and aspiring entrepreneurs that are trusting God to direct their paths in their business endeavors. As you read this book remember that you have been permitted to prosper!

Permission to Prosper

A 31 – Day Devotional for Business Owners

This devotional is dedicated to Christian business owners and entrepreneurs who strive day after day to excel in their business. I want you to know I see your struggles, as I'm well acquainted with the challenges we all face in our businesses and pursuits. My desire and prayer for you are the same as the words of John the Apostle; *'Beloved, I pray that in every way you may succeed and prosper and be in good health [physically], just as [I know] your soul prospers [spiritually].' – 3rd John 2 AMP.*

This devotional holds inspired words of counsel, divine strategies, and some wisdom you might need for your business growth or recovery. I encourage you to take a few minutes to pray after reading the words for each day, asking God for guidance, counsel, and wisdom in your business endeavors. As you read this with an open heart, may the power of the Holy Spirit quicken your mind and supply you with fresh, innovative, straight–from–heaven ideas for your business.

All the best to you and have a fruitful reading!

Gicele

TABLE OF CONTENTS

WEEK 1 – WHY GOD WANTS US WEALTHY

Day 1

'Seek first the kingdom of God and His righteousness, and all these things shall be added to you.'
– Matthew 6:33 NKJV

As business owners, it is first important that we understand why God would be interested in helping us succeed in our business. We need to realize that the world – *every part of it* – is run by two kingdoms: The Eternal Kingdom of Christ and the temporal kingdom of the devil, and there is a heavy contention on both sides on who will get to control the treasures of the earth. Remember the devil's temptation of Christ, when he showed him all the kingdoms of this world and promised to give them to Him? (See Luke 4:5-8) Now, if the old devil would not give his false treasures to Christ without first getting a commitment from Him, do you think God would give His true wealth to us without our loyalty and commitment to His kingdom?

Our Bible verse for today answers the question for us. Making God's kingdom a priority is one of the keys to recovery, growth, and establishment of our businesses, as God blesses *primarily* for His kingdom's sake. You're either serving God with your means, or you'll end up worshipping your means. When you put *God's kingdom first*, giving heartily toward its advancement, and favoring His priorities, you will encounter kingdom wealth.

'My cities shall again spread out through prosperity; the Lord will again comfort Zion.' – Zechariah 1:17.

Develop a heart *filled with passion* for the things of God, for without it you cannot make a mark on the earth. Don't keep your gold away from God, rather serve Him with it and watch Him as He multiplies your substance supernaturally!

Day 2

'And you shall remember the LORD your God, for it is He who gives you the power to get wealth, that He may establish His covenant which He swore to your fathers, as it is this day.'
— Deuteronomy 8:18 NKJV

As sons of God's kingdom, and as seeds of Abraham through faith in Christ (See Galatians 3:29), God's covenant of prosperity remains true and valid *today,* and the way it plays out is that God gives us – *not money* – but the supernatural ability to get it. He opens our eyes to see what others are not seeing, He gives us the power and the wisdom that gets wealth and gives us favor with men. In other words, when we are in the right alignment with His ways, we won't have to struggle and sweat hard just to enjoy success in our businesses and careers. God is the author of true riches. He holds in His hands the power to make wealth but only gives this power to those who serve Him with all their hearts and place His kingdom above all else. Too often, the enemy lies and makes people think that God is against wealth.

Well, *no*! God is only against greed and covetousness. He delights in seeing His people prosper in everything – which includes finances! Jesus, in His days on earth as a physical man, prospered in His finances. He never went around broke, borrowing and begging from family, friends, or banks. You know why? He was living His life for God's kingdom and glory, He was fully committed to His Father and this secured Him supernatural favor from heaven, all that He needed was fully supplied by God's hand!

You are destined to succeed in your business, but it's your alignment with God's priorities that secures your portion for you. It does not matter whatever business you're doing, as long as you're trying to build an honest and life-impacting business, God's touch can transform it and make it good!

Day 3

'If they obey and serve Him, they shall spend their days in prosperity, and their years in pleasures.'
– Job 36:11 NKJV

God prospers those who serve Him wholeheartedly and prepares the pleasures of godly satisfaction and contentment for them. However, it is not His desire that what He gives should start and end *with you alone,* but to extend to future generations – starting from your children!

Legacy involves a deliberate living and aiming to build into generations to come for their wellness and success. It is more than – but often includes money and assets/properties. I know it might sound far-fetched and unrealistic for some reading this, *but it is possible* for your struggling or growing business to attain the greatness needed to set you on a path to setting a legacy for the future.

'The righteous man walks in his integrity; **his children are blessed after him**.' *– Proverbs 20:7*

Never you despise your current state because if you serve the Lord Christ and trust in Him for wisdom, and daily learn to commit your business into His hands, I assure you He will work wonders with it!

Day 4

'Praise the Lord! Blessed is the man who fears the Lord, who delights greatly in His commandments. His descendants will be mighty on earth; the generation of the upright will be blessed. Wealth and riches will be in his house, and his righteousness endures forever.'
– Psalm 112:1-3 NKJV

'Get wisdom! Get understanding!' cries the voice of the Holy Spirit in the Scriptures (See Proverbs 4:5). In your pursuit to establish or expand your business, you need to know that God's design is always made to last. He made just one sun and moon and they've been hanging up in the sky for thousands of years. All the physical things He made were once and for all, He never needed to create them again after a few years. He made *even you* last for all eternity!

'When He prepared the heavens, I was there, when He drew a circle on the face of the deep when He established the clouds above. Then I was beside Him as a master craftsman; and I was daily His delight, rejoicing always before Him. Rejoicing in His inhabited world, and my delight was with the sons of men.' – Proverbs 8:27,30,31.

Of course, you will not be able to make anything that will last for eternity – and no man will – but here's my point: we must, by God's grace and wisdom, seek to build what will last. Beyond *now,* beyond *tomorrow*, we must determine to build what will still be in existence when we leave the earth. I'm sure you'd love to build a business that your grandkids could benefit from, even after you're gone. Do you think it's impossible?

'Now to Him who is able to do exceedingly abundantly above all that we ask or think, according to the power that works in us...' – Ephesians 3:20

When you pray, pray big! Trust big and plan big. It might not be easy, but it will be worth it. You might need to take a longer and much tougher path but if you endure, you will achieve your goal.

Just remember that you have been permitted to prosper!

Day 5

'Now acquaint yourself with Him and be at peace; thereby good shall come to you. Then you will lay your gold in the dust, and the gold of Ophir among the stones of the brooks. Yes, the Almighty will be your gold and your precious silver.'
– Job 22: 21,24,25 NKJV

Here is an ancient secret known and practiced by two of the greatest businessmen in the Bible, Abraham, and Job. They understood that God is not committed to those who are not committed to Him but has great rewards for those who serve Him committedly. They also understood that no matter how much wealth or level of success attained, earthly wealth is temporal, and God is the real gold. God was a treasure to them, they loved Him, served Him, and obeyed Him wholeheartedly (See Genesis 22:13-19, Job 1:1, Job 42:10-12).

These two men had a few things in common; First, they both knew God and regarded Him as the Almighty who owns the heavens and the earth; Second, they were both extremely wealthy; Third, they both left great legacies for their posterity. These two men's lives demonstrate to us that an extraordinarily strong relationship with Christ is a foundation for a successful business.

If you walk in the steps of Abraham and Job, walking righteously before God, having reverence for His name, listening for His voice and obeying every instruction He gives you – though I cannot promise that you'll become the wealthiest man in your community or the most successful business in town (as that largely depends on so many factors) – one thing I can assure you of is that you will *never* be down in your business. God has promised to prosper the works of the righteous and the same holds true for you! (See Psalm 1:1-3).

Day 6

'Calling ten of his servants, he gave them ten minas, and said to them, 'Engage in business until I come.'
– Luke 19:13 NKJV

It is God's will that His people prosper in business – but beyond that – He also desires that we occupy important positions in the society. There are a lot of sectors in the society that are waiting for God's people to step up and occupy – even though the enemy might resist this at first. The thing is you need to develop the mindset of a man on a mission, see yourself as an agent for God's kingdom who has been sent for a divine purpose – it will interest you to know that's how the devil sees you anyway, which explains why he will try to put up a fight and resist your initial advances.

Christ needs His people to arise and engage in business (governmental leadership and even international leadership) until He returns. He wants to invade both the government and the private sectors and begin to place His people in key positions. He wants Christian businesses to dominate the corporate world, helping to give expression to the riches that Christ has secured through His sacrificial death and victorious resurrection.

'Worthy is the Lamb who was slain to receive power and riches and wisdom and strength and honor and glory and blessing!' – Revelation 5:12.

Someone is reading this, and the Lord is saying to you that He has a plan to use you in amazing ways far beyond your business – your destiny will take you through the corporate world where the Lord will cause you to make waves and create great impact – and if you're faithful and stay in fellowship with Him, He's going to promote you and move you over into the realm of international/political leadership so He can use you as a vessel to paralyze the games of satan among political leaders and exalt the banner of righteousness!

Satan hates the sons of God and does all he can to stop us from occupying the positions of wealth and influence that Christ has prepared for us, but the devil is not the problem – he remains *forever* defeated by the blood of the Lamb. We are the ones who will rise up in the name of the Lord and in the power of His Spirit and take that which belongs to us. When we take our place as God's sons, the evil powers that look to withstand and oppose God's plan for our lives will give way.

Day 7

"The silver is mine, the gold is mine," says the LORD of hosts.
– Haggai 2:8 NKJV

The devil likes to boast and make people believe that he alone can give them riches, and so there are many businesses out there who have aligned themselves with satan so they could get what he offers. This is a Christian devotional so I'm going to tell you the truth; the devil does make *his* people rich, but he doesn't own the riches – he only steals them and diverts them to those who serve him! His riches are *counterfeit* and they come with sorrows, oppression, and depression. They plunge the souls of men into deep darkness and make them slaves of sin!

True riches come from God, and He delights in prospering those who serve Him. However, God's gold and silver are not given to those whom the Lord has not tested. You will have to pass the test of faithfulness before you will be entrusted with heaven's wealth. You want your business to fly high? The secret is this: serve God with all your heart, obey Him in all things, and love His kingdom. God owns the gold and the silver, and those among His kingdom-minded people will grow increasingly prosperous. I'm yet to see anyone who *sincerely* loves the Lord and doesn't prosper in his business. However, God doesn't want us to come to Him because of His wealth – although these will be supernaturally added to us when we seek first His kingdom and righteousness — but because He is everything to us.

Day 8

'No servant can serve two masters; for either he will hate the one and love the other, or else he will be loyal to the one and despise the other. You cannot serve God and mammon.'
– Luke 16:13 NKJV

These very words of Christ tell us of the danger of seeking financial prosperity or breakthrough for our businesses without having God's interests at heart. There is an evil power (mammon) that uses money/success to contest with God's place in your life. This evil power makes people get greedy for money, he works the love of money into the souls of men, and by it, he controls their thoughts and influences their emotions.

If the idea of money is euphoric to you – or you spend most of your time thinking and strategizing on how to make more money – you're probably under the influence of mammon, at least in some measure. Mammon likes to make people discontented with the things they have and makes them covetous for more and more, but God would have none of that! Rather He wants His people to be under the influence of the Holy Spirit. So, in your quest for success in your business, you must open up your heart to God and ask Him to purify your heart!

'And He said to them, "Take heed and beware of covetousness, for one's life does not consist in the abundance of the things he possesses.' – Luke 12;15

20

Another way to describe the manifestation of mammon is *'money without a kingdom mission.'* People who want to have money or succeed in business just so they can acquire more possessions are under the influence of mammon. God's desire for us is to extricate ourselves from being under the influence of this spirit and the twisted system it has created. To fully experience heaven's economy, we must clean up our lives and rid the enemy of any opportunity to influence like he does those who belong to the world.

WEEK 2 – THE PLACE OF DILIGENCE

Day 9

*'And I have filled him with the Spirit of God, with ability and
intelligence, with knowledge and all craftsmanship, to devise
artistic designs, to work in gold, silver, and bronze, in cutting
stones for setting, and in carving wood, to work in every craft.'*
– Exodus 31:3-5 NKJV

Since we prioritize the anointing of God's Spirit over skill
and professional ability, yet there is a place of getting
the necessary skills in our areas of business. If skill
weren't important, God would simply have sent His
angels to create the equipment in the tabernacle of
Moses. But instead, He takes some men by the names
of Bezalel and Ahisamach, and supernaturally imparts
them with the spirit of wisdom, giving them the skill to
work, make designs and get things done artistically *or
professionally.*

However, God didn't mean the skills He had imparted to
these men to be for them alone – He wanted them to
teach others – so He also gave them both the ability to
teach others who would be interested in learning from
them (See Exodus 35:34). You see, if someone is
anointed in an area, then some level of skill should go
with the anointing! I'm sure you wouldn't want to engage

in any business dealings with someone who is anointed but lacks the necessary skills in his field, or would you?

Whether you are a Christian artist, an athlete, a trader, a businessman, medical personnel, or a schoolteacher, prioritize the things of the Spirit, but also get the needed skills in your area of business or profession. There is no end to learning – much like water never fills a basket, no matter how much water you pour into it. Here's how King Solomon puts it:

'A wise man will hear and increase learning, and a man of understanding will attain wise counsel.' – Proverbs 1:5.

Day after day, technology advances at a crazy rate. Discoveries are being made, some of which require us to unlearn the former things and learn new things. Indeed, our God never changes (See Malachi 3:6, Hebrews 13:8), but we live in a changing world and must keep up with the changes – as long as it doesn't harm our faith in Christ and our commitment to His Kingdom.

Day 10

'Let a man so consider us, as servants of Christ and stewards of the mysteries of God. Moreover, it is found in stewards that one be found faithful.'
– 1 Corinthians 4:1,2 NKJV

Talking about business success, the need for wisdom, the need for diligence, and giving, without talking about stewardship would be incomplete. Stewardship – *the responsible and careful management of resources entrusted into one's care* – is a special responsibility between a man and his Lord. A good steward is not one who has been entrusted with certain resources and then waits for people to determine how he dispenses it. *NO.* Rather, he is one who looks to his Master for direction as to how best to utilize that which has given into his hands.

Many business owners only want God's blessings and favor upon their struggling or growing businesses but are not ready to become His stewards. They want to have it all to themselves, and never think about giving except the offering plate is passed at church or someone gets in deep trouble and needs some help. If you believe God for a blessing and He comes through for you, and then you forget Him momentarily, do you think He could trust you enough as to commit great amounts of resources into your hands?

Many times, God tests us with little things – as He did with Joseph in the house of Potiphar – to see if we would be faithful. Joseph's faithful stewardship was what earned him a throne in Egypt, so if you want to achieve success and have some impact in the business world, by God's grace, be faithful. Give when He tells you to give, *and give what He wants you to give,* - whether food, money, clothing or some other personal possession. Don't hoard and try to justify it as planning for the future when God's Spirit is moving in your heart, anything He doesn't say to put in a saving's plan should be used to presently support His kingdom. Remember, obedience to His leading will bring about a supernatural replenishment to your purse!

Day 11

'Not lagging in diligence, fervent in spirit, serving the Lord,
distributing to the needs of the saints, given to hospitality.'
– Romans 12:11,13 NKJV

The keywords in our Bible verse for today are these: *diligence, fervent, serving, distributing, and hospitality.*

You cannot achieve *anything* in this world without being diligent, it as a discipline we must cultivate. You must consistently pursue your dreams and refuse to be deterred by any mountain that stands between you and your ultimate goal.

One of the things that help to overcome barriers is developing and maintaining a fervent spirit. This is achieved through the habitual practice of fasting and prayer, I tell you the truth – this could save you from making wrong investments! When you're given to regular fasting and praying, you will be spiritually sensitive to know when danger lies ahead and how to avoid it. When things are not going smoothly as you desire, get into fasting, and praying. As you do this, God's supernatural power will be released to work on your behalf. So, as busy as you might be, create time for fasting and prayer – at least weekly.

Did you know that John D. Rockefeller, America's first billionaire, was a churchwarden? There is a blessing that comes with serving in God's house, it helps us in humbling our hearts before God, it reminds us that no matter how much possession or money we have – we are still God's sheep and He is our shepherd. Serving the Lord gets Him interested *and involved* in all that we lay our hands upon!

Serving the Lord is more than just attending weekly services – it also includes sharing our substance with fellow believers who are in need. When you distribute to the needs of fellow Christians, and you open your heart to helping strangers, you're setting yourself up for promotion in God's economy! Abraham got himself a blessing when he opened up his heart to strangers, he washed their feet and fed them with good food. That was the day God finally spoke and promised to give bless his household with a son! (Genesis 18:1-15).

Day 12

"He who loves pleasure will be a poor man; he who loves wine and oil will not be rich."
— Proverbs 21:17 NKJV

The system of the world drives many people to live a lavish and extravagant life. Some people have a remarkably high taste, even though they have an incredibly low income. In an attempt to impress family, friends [and even strangers] who do not care about them, they love to purchase expensive stuff they don't need, and then it becomes a habit that gets difficult to break. Much of the money spent on acquiring those things could be used for something more meaningful.

Similarly, impulse buying digs a hole in the pocket of those who are in the habit. We must be very careful and self-controlled in the things we buy; we must not allow our eyes or our flesh to decide what we spend money on. It's okay to ask yourself these kinds of questions before making purchases: Do I need it? How will it add any benefits to the growth and expansion of my business? Will it help enhance my finances personally? Will it get me more customers or clients? What are the advantages and disadvantages? etc.

We must discipline our eyes and tame our flesh and refuse to let them get us into trouble. Learning to deny the flesh holds many benefits, and yes, these include financial benefits. You might have heard of great men who lost their greatness because they were given to fleshly pleasures, they loved women, they loved wine, they loved food, they loved partying. Such men lacked the wisdom and self-control of Daniel who purposed in his heart that he would not defile himself with the portion of the king's delicacies, nor with the wine which he drank (See Daniel 1:8).

Day 13

'How long will you slumber, O sluggard? When will you rise from your sleep? A little sleep, a little slumber, a little folding of the hands to sleep – so shall your poverty come on you like a prowler and your need like an armed man.'
– Proverbs 6:9-11 NKJV

If you seek to excel in business, you must understand that you need to be *very* diligent and must be disciplined with the way you sleep. The reason why many people struggle in business and are not able to come up with innovative ideas is *simply* because of bad sleeping habits. Oversleeping [which could also be as a result of overeating or spending too much time in front of the TV] has robbed many of the precious time they could otherwise have channeled into prayer, meditation, and productive thinking!

Cultivate the discipline of getting up from sleep during the night, or in the early hours of the morning – just to be alone so you can pray, meditate, and think. I have received a lot of ideas and inspiration from heaven this way, so I'm telling you what works! Choose a time that works best for you and use it – just make sure the time you chose will have everyone else in the house sleeping. This is one of the secrets of Jesus' success (See Mark 1:35-37), and I tell you the truth – if it worked for the Lord's ministry in His days in Israel, it will work for you!

Day 14

'This book of the law shall not depart from your mouth, but you shall meditate in it day and night, that you may observe to do according to all that is written in it. For then you will make your way prosperous, and then you will have good success.'
– Joshua 1:8 NKJV.

One of God's standard formulas for success is presented here in the above Bible verse, but unfortunately many just skim right over it and never pay serious attention to it. Meditation is almost as powerful as prayer, it does a lot of work in our inner being and imparts the wisdom of God into our hearts. Besides, God does not only speak in prayer, He also speaks to us in meditation. When we meditate on and speak the word of God from a heart full of revelation and faith, mountains on our paths will either shift or God would show us the way around them!

Isaac was a wealthy man, he never had anyone prophecy over him, but he had a habit of going to a quiet place to meditate on the things he knew about God (See Genesis 24:63). Meditation on God's word will do you a whole lot of good – beyond financial success. The bible verse in Joshua 1:8 says, 'good success', and that means it's going to be an all-round success. You will not only be prosperous but also healthy in your body and wise in your heart.

Do you want success in your business? Then *'Meditate on these things; give yourself entirely to them, that your progress may be evident to all.'* *– 1 Timothy 4:15.*

Day 15

"Go to the ants, thou sluggard; consider her ways and be wise. Which, having no captain, overseer or ruler, provides her supplies in the summer and gathers her food in the harvest."
– Proverbs 6:6-8 NKJV

God points to nature several times in the scriptures and tells us to learn valuable lessons from them. However, it is almost impossible to understand animal language. So, since we can't have verbal communication together – then we are forced to only observe them and learn good lessons from their behaviors. If God tells us to learn from animals, then I believe He also wants us to learn from each other.

There are a few people in some other parts of the world who have *probably* attempted what you're involved with. Some of them are long dead, while some are still alive today. While some of them failed big, some achieved a small amount of success, and some others exploded in triumph – but I tell you, you will find golden lessons to learn from each one of them. One thing about reading the works and adventures of other folks is that it teaches you *natural* wisdom, it encourages you to keep on keeping on, it warns you to avoid the mistakes they made, and it challenges you to achieve more than they did!

So, get books and other study materials about people you want to learn from. Then you need to dedicate quality time to studying, meditation, and finding out what you want to know.

Bildad, one of Job's wise friends, puts it this way: *'For inquire, please, of the former age, and consider the things discovered by their fathers, for we were born yesterday, and know nothing because our days on earth are a shadow. Will they not teach you and tell you, and utter words from their heart?' – Job 8:8-10.*

When you humble yourself and learn from others, then you will discover there are many treasures to be discovered and who knows? You just might find the answer to your questions!

Day 16

'He who has a slack hand becomes poor, but the hand of the diligent makes rich. He who gathers in summer is a wise son, he who sleeps in harvest is a son who causes shame.'
– Proverbs 10:4,5 NKJV

No one is born poor, and no one is born rich. Nobody was born with a 3-piece suit on, with a designer wristwatch and expensive shoes. Everyone came the same way, and none carried a checkbook or a purse along with him from the womb. People arrive here on earth to become whatever they choose to be.

Just in a moment, I want you to see the balance between giving and working. *Giving procures the blessings and opens your heavens while working opens the channel through which the blessings to you.* Giving gets God committed to your financial wellness, while your work shows your readiness and capacity to receive His blessings on your life. Giving without being diligent with your work or business is like pouring water into a basket! Know this today; *God hates laziness*! The scriptures teach against laziness and encourage God's people to work with their hands!

Abraham the father of faith encountered the promise of blessings by giving, but he experienced the blessings by working; he was a cattle rearer! Isaac worked, Jacob worked, Job worked – and these men were all men of faith. They understood the place of giving, but they were also diligent in business!

If you will keep giving, and you will keep being diligent in business, there is no way you won't flourish in the end. In all labor, there is profit (See Proverbs 14:23). So, make sure your hands remain working hands because working hands are blessed hands!

WEEK 3 – WHAT WE NEED TO KNOW ABOUT GIVING

Day 17

'The blessing of the Lord makes one rich, and He adds no sorrow with it.'
– Proverbs 10:22 NKJV

There is a place where wealth comes from, and it is the mouth of the Lord – through His blessings! We need to secure the Lord's blessing, and although it is hidden to the physical eyes, it is nonetheless real. The world often paints a false picture and gives a false promise of prosperity to those who work hard. While it is important to be diligent in business and do what you need to do, as kingdom people you must also understand that struggling is not God's plan for you, neither is it God's way of prospering His people.

The Bible teaches us in many ways, such as giving us instructions, principles, or amazingly simple stories or parables. God teaches us an important lesson through Peter's story, which shows us this truth more vividly. In Luke 5:1-7, we read of how Peter struggled all through the night hoping to catch a few fish – may be just enough to sell and feed his family with – but the more he tried, the faster the fish all ran away from him. But then Jesus steps in and gave him His word of blessing and counsel, bringing Peter so much than he could handle

One other reason why we must secure the Lord's blessing — and stop struggling hard to make it — is that it solves not only our challenges but also that of others with us. Peter had his business partners with him, and they were in their other boat. They too had worked all night without achieving success — but when the Lord spoke and commanded Peter's blessing — Peter invited them to come over and help with the astonishing success he had just encountered!

Do you see the lesson in that story? While we must develop the necessary skills and acquire good equipment, always remember this — it is the blessing of the Lord that makes His people rich, and not their struggles!

Day 18

"Come now, and let us reason together,' says the LORD... 'If you are willing and obedient, you shall eat the good of the land.'
– Isaiah 1:18,19 NKJV

Like most businesspeople often experience, there often comes a season when we get stuck and we need a trusted friend we could get some counsel and encouragement from. One of the best ways to get through such seasons is to find some quiet place – with your bible, a journal, and a pen – where you could talk to God. Get a hundred percent transparent with Him, I mean, open up your heart and tell Him the difficult situation your business is going through. Ask Him to counsel you and show you the way out.

He wants the best for you – whether you believe it or not. As you speak to Him, listen for what He will say and make sure to write them down in your journal. Be prepared for whatever, because His counsel might sound crazy, unbelievable, or unrealistic; but I assure you, if you would simply obey Him, something *really* good is going to happen to you!

Day 19

"Give, and it will be given to you: good measure, pressed down, shaken together, and running over will be put into your bosom."
– Luke 6:38 NKJV

As the nations of the earth depend heavily on their economy, always working to make sure it is healthy knowing that their well-being and prosperity depend on it, even so, heaven has its economy – for the people of God. The beautiful thing is heaven's economy does not suffer recession of any kind. There is abundance for everyone, for every kingdom business, and every family.

Now, the reason why many Christians, businesses, and families suffer financial difficulty is that they do not know *how* to access what heaven has made available to them. Have you heard the term before, '*Open heavens'?* Whether your answer is yes or no, open heavens simply refer to God's favor being released upon your finances and other areas of your life!

If there is such a thing as open heavens, then there must be keys to get it opened, right? Jesus tells us one of the keys to accessing heaven's economy is giving! Are you fed up with being small and suffering limitations in your business? Then give your way out of that situation! Again, Israel's wisest and wealthiest king, Solomon, tells us a secret that will work for anyone who believes.

'Honour the Lord with your possessions, and with the first fruits of all your increase; so your barns will be filled

with plenty, and your vats will overflow with new wine.'
– Proverbs 3:9,10.

Please understand I'm not trying to relieve you of your hard-earned money, I'm only trying to show you keys that will open your heavens and bring down God's favor upon all that you lay your hands upon. Do you know why you need these keys? It's pretty simple: No kingdom business can flourish without aligning itself under heaven's economy!

Day 20

'There is one who scatters yet increases more, and there is one who withholds more than is right, but it leads to poverty.'
— Proverbs 11:24 NKJV

When you keep your substance away from God, it is to your hurt! God's word is plain and easy to understand, if He says your generosity is a key to your financial increase, then He means just that. Don't think that God is after your substance, He's only after your heart. Those who hold back from God will not experience His supernatural power in provision. Listen to the words of one of the wisest and wealthiest men that ever lived, King Solomon:

'There is a severe evil which I have seen under the sun: riches kept for their owner to his hurt.'
— Ecclesiastes 5:13

There is the story of the wealthy man who hoarded his substance, he refused to share his substance with those in desperate need, he wanted to have it all to himself but he ends up losing it all (See 1 Samuel 25). One reason why people hoard their substance is so they could gratify the needs of their flesh, but you see, delayed gratification has a lot of hidden benefits, and those who cultivate this beautiful habit will be more blessed and fruitful in their business than those who don't.

In the same sense, those who hoard money disqualify themselves from heaven's economy, it is those who distribute money freely that God blesses with it. Jesus teaches us to be rich toward God and serve Him with all that we have (See Luke 12:15). When you open your hands to others, God opens His large hands to you; and when you shut your hands to others, God shuts His big hands to you – it's pretty simple, isn't it?

Day 21

'And he blessed him and said: Blessed be Abram of God Most High, possessor of heaven and earth; and blessed be God Most High, who has delivered your enemy into your hands. And he gave him a tithe of all.'
— Genesis 15:19,20 NKJV

We read of Abraham, a businessman, in the pages of the Bible; and we also read of his children down to the fourth generation who ended up in Egypt through Joseph. All these people were blessed and favored of the Lord because of Abraham's singular act of giving a tithe to the Priest-King of Salem, Melchizedek.

I understand many doctrines are flying around concerning the payment or non-payment of the tithe, and in this writing, I offer my perspective of the benefits of tithing and giving. Abraham the father of faith paid tithe and he got a blessing from heaven; we also need to be faithful in tithing if we want heavens resources to be released to us. I need you to understand what the bottom line is: Giving! It does not matter the religious or doctrinal label we put on it, what matters is the act and heart of giving to advance God's purposes. Paul tells us that God loves a cheerful giver and will not withhold His blessings from them (See 2 Corinthians 9:5-10).

When we give *consistently* to God's purposes and the interests of His Kingdom, He speaks and opens the heavens over our businesses. Even more, He releases upon us divine ideas and strategies that can shift our lives and businesses to the next level.

Day 22

'In the morning sow your seed, and in the evening do not withhold your hand; for you do not know which will prosper, either this or that, or whether both alike will be good.'
– Ecclesiastes 11:6 NKJV

There are many blessings and rewards for the open-handed businessman/woman and the entrepreneur. Of course, I am not suggesting wasteful or uncontrolled spending, rather I am referring to a planned and deliberate giving *of your substance* to others. (Giving is not limited to money alone, you could also give a gift, an act of service, your time and also words of encouragement). When we give, it enlarges our hearts and makes it much easier to receive ideas and guidance from God. This is because God is delighted when we open our hands to give to the needs of other people, and He will work out a way to reward our good deeds.

So, remember this always: Be open-handed to the needy as much as you can – often share your meal with the hungry – give those unused clothes to someone who needs it – and watch as God rewards you. Every good deed is a seed that the Lord will bless!

Day 23

"He that gives to the poor shall not lack."
– Proverbs 28:27 NKJV

Giving to the poor is one of the ways we secure heaven's attention and get God to be involved in our financial prosperity and business growth. I understand this might be a bit hard to swallow, especially since it cannot be proven scientifically or *economically* but that's the way of heaven, and that's the way of faith. Remember, we are a spiritual people and we believe in the simplicity and *seeming* foolishness of the word of God. Besides, the foolishness of God is wiser than the most educated of men (See 1 Corinthians 1:25).

God blesses us so that we can give to the needy, helping to feed them, clothe them, and help pay their bills. Just go ahead and commit to doing something for the poor if you want to see the hand of God move in your favor. God is faithful and can *never* break His word, as He says in another place in the scriptures: *'He who keeps the commandment keeps his soul, but he who is careless of his ways will die. He who pities the poor* lends *to the Lord, and He will pay back what he has given.' – Proverbs 19:17.*

When you give to the poor and meet their needs when you lend a hand in delivering the hungry from their hunger pangs, you *lend* to the Lord, and He won't be ungrateful. He will show you His gratitude by repaying you with His favor and blessings, with some bonus. You

47

don't need a big fat bank account to give to the poor, all you need is a large heart that *always* includes the less privileged in its budgets.

Day 24

'My thoughts are not your thoughts, nor are your ways My ways,'
says the Lord. For as the heavens are higher than the earth, so are
My ways higher than your ways, and My thoughts than your
thoughts.'
– Isaiah 55:8,9 NKJV

Christ is an eternal King, and if Christians know Him as we should, our businesses should have a touch of eternity. Your business is not allowed to be the same as that of the unbeliever who is all about making money. Are you just in business for survival? Just to put food on your table and some clothes for your family? And a nice car? That's okay if that's all you want, but God calls you to something higher! Like Abraham, He wants you to be a blessing to many others. He wants lives to be changed for the better through your business.

Christ has a different way, *and a different motive,* for us to do business, and it is far different from what is taught in many business schools. He expects His people's lives and businesses to be another frontier for the expansion of His kingdom. He wants your business to touch lives and make them better

WEEK 4 – WALKING IN HEAVENLY WISDOM

Day 25

'A good man leaves an inheritance to his children's children, but the wealth of the sinner is stored up for the righteous.'
– Proverbs 13:22 NKJV

One of the blessings we need most in our lives is the supernatural impartation of wisdom. We need this if we're going to build anything worthwhile. Your business, marriage, and personal life all need the wisdom to excel at whatever you do. When wisdom fills your heart and helps in guiding your business affairs, you will understand the importance of building a business that will last for at least a century.

If you build a business that only works while you're alive, it means all you worked for was for your own temporal needs. A close study of scriptures shows us that all who served the Lord in their times never left the earth without leaving a rich legacy behind. We have the stories of Abraham, Jacob, and Job as men who all left legacies behind for their posterity – both spiritual and material/financial legacies.

I encourage you to dream high, plan solid and aspire to build business empires that will outlast you. Look to build more than a business or a brand. By God's help, build a business that will transmit a legacy of prosperity to future generations!

Day 26

'I, wisdom, dwell with prudence, and find out knowledge of witty inventions.'
– Proverbs 8:12 KJV.

Whatever area of the business world you are called to, you need to realize that you need the pure wisdom of heaven. This is because you cannot create anything long-lasting outside of wisdom. You see, the wisdom by which God created all things is the simple reason why all that He made has not expired even after thousands of years, and that's why you wake up every morning and see the sunrise and set *day after day*, you see the stars shine each in its course and you see the rain and snow come down in their seasons – and it's been happening *consistently* that way for thousands of years; it's the same reason why God's creation does not need any kind of upgrade (See Genesis 1) because all that He made is perfect and does not need man's improvements.

'When He prepared the heavens, I was there, when He drew a circle on the face of the deep when He established the clouds above. Then I was beside Him as a master craftsman; and I was daily His delight, rejoicing always before Him. Rejoicing in His inhabited world, and my delight was with the sons of men.' – Proverbs 8:27,30,31.

If God could create nothing without wisdom, neither can you! You need to get down on your knees often and ask

Him to fill your heart with wisdom (See James 1:5,6,17), so you can win in business and get solutions to complex problems!

Day 27

'That I may cause those who love me to inherit wealth, that I may fill their treasuries.'
– Proverbs 8:18-21 NKJV

There is no money in heaven – not even a single dime or else Jesus would have *freely* given lots of it to every Christian in this world – because He's quite generous! All the money we need is down here on the earth, and the devil is trying to control it all. But he isn't supposed to control your money except you let him.

Though money is man-made and physical, it's direction can be determined in the spirit/supernatural realm. Amazingly, some people usually think that wealth can be stumbled upon accidentally, while others think that their hard work *alone* can get them the needed wealth. However, the possibility of both mindsets is very slim. It's nice to daydream and keep wishing that money would fall out of the sky – if that's okay with you – please keep it up; and it's exceptionally good to work hard and develop strong work ethics.

Here's my point: there is no guarantee – whether in heaven or on earth – that daydreaming and hard work will amount to wealth or success in business. However, there is a sure path to wealth, and this is the path of wisdom! You're invited to walk on this path because there you will find counsel, understanding, and fail-proof strategies that will yield amazing results!

Day 28

"To everything, there is a season, and a time for every purpose under heaven: A time to plant and a time to pluck what is planted. A time to break down and a time to build up"
— Ecclesiastes 3:1-3 NKJV

Life is in cycles and seasons, and this affects every area of our lives. Doing the right thing in the wrong season is going to lead to failure (like planting summer crops in winter and vice-versa) while doing the wrong thing at the right season will likewise lead to failure and disappointment. This is a fact that Christian entrepreneurs must get right! Farmers know this truth more than anyone else; that different crops grow in different seasons – and it's not just about artificial irrigation – but about the fact that each crop flourishes under its *favorable* climatic conditions.

Some crops grow in winter, such as spinach, carrots, cabbage, turnip, onions, etc. and there are others than only do well in the warm climate of summer such as cucumbers, muskmelons, eggplant, basil, squash, garlic, etc. The oppressive heat of summer has its blessings, much like the bitter cold of winter has its own too.

Whatever you're creating or selling, you need to understand that seasons will always affect your business. There are times when people are extremely happy, and there are times when they are just sad, some seasons are more productive while others seem wasteful and meaningless. Much like crops, humans have their seasons – each individual with his own. You must prayerfully observe the seasons that God has prepared for you and trust Him for wisdom on how to maximize them.

The Bible tells us of some of God's people and how they discerned the times and seasons, *'of the sons of Issachar who had an understanding of the times, to know what Israel ought to do.' – 1 Chronicle 12:32.* There are a time and a place to do business, and there's a time to simply observe and wait. Like the sons of Issachar, may we be wise and discerning of the right and wrong seasons for us *as individuals*, so you don't put your money on wasteful investments.

Day 29

'Why is there in the hand of a fool the purchase price of wisdom since he has no heart for it?'
— Proverbs 17:16 NKJV

Getting wisdom is not as difficult as many think, people just have difficulties with paying the price. Purchasing anything of great value in a store requires you to pay some amount of hard-earned money, right? Yes, and so there is a price for wisdom – and that price is this: *a burning desire in your heart and relentless determination to find wisdom!* (See Proverbs 2:1-6). Wisdom is not far from people.

'Does not wisdom cry out and understanding lift up her voice? To you, O men, I call, and my voice is to the sons of men.' – Proverbs 8:1,4.

Wisdom is *always* looking for someone's heart to fill, and someone's life to use as an instrument of expression. When wisdom finds a heart full of desire and is relentless in its pursuit, a partnership is then formed between the divine and the human, between the supernatural and the natural.

Wisdom will teach how to save costs, how to maximize your budget, and how best to make a profit from your business dealings. May I suggest that you should take some time to read the eight chapters of the book of Proverbs? This will give you a much fuller understanding of the things that wisdom can do in the life of those who possess it.

Day 30

'Trust in the LORD with all your heart and lean not on your own understanding. In all your ways acknowledge Him, and He shall direct all your paths.'
– Proverbs 3:5-6 NKJV

Learning to trust God is important in our lives and our businesses. This means *to depend wholly on Him and to have no other alternatives.* Quite some people believe God, but only a very few trust Him. Some so many people give worship offerings in church but have never enjoyed the favor of God in their businesses or finances. Do you know why? They are in no way dependent on God for their needs, instead, they depend on their pay packets, on their big brothers, or their rich friends.

Thus says the Lord: "Cursed is the man who trusts in man and makes flesh his strength, whose heart departs from the Lord. For he shall be like a shrub in the desert, and shall not see when good comes, but shall inhabit the parched places in the wilderness, in a salt land which is not inhabited. "Blessed is the man who trusts in the Lord, and whose hope is the Lord. For he shall be like a tree planted by the waters, Which spreads out its roots by the river, and will not fear when heat comes; But its leaf will be green, and will not be anxious in the year of drought, nor will cease from yielding fruit.' – Jeremiah 17:5

But God would have no rival – He wants to get all the glory for Himself – and the sooner you begin to trust

God, the sooner you'll get to experience His faithfulness in helping you establishing or expanding your business. Learn to take God at His word, keep believing His promises, and be relentless in your pursuit. The realm of trusting God is the realm of continuous triumph, so when you set your whole heart on His ability to help you reach your goals, or to help you succeed in whatever needs to be done, you're sure going to experience His help.

One of the things that command people's trust and influence their emotions is money. When people's souls are tied to their money, they allow money to break their relationships with wonderful people, they let money determine who qualifies to be their friend and who doesn't, they let money decide the tempo of their spiritual life, but God does not bring multiplication the way of such people. Beloved, don't put your trust in money, it can fail you (Genesis 47:15), rather put your trust in God! Don't trust in your wisdom, trust in God's wisdom. Take away your eyes from your rich relatives or friends – stop hoping on them. If you believe that God owns the silver and the gold, then trusting Him should be fun – *and indeed it is fun* – and fruitful!

Day 31

'Riches and honor are with me, enduring riches and righteousness. My fruit is better than gold, and my revenue than choice silver.'
— Proverbs 8: 18-19 NKJV

It is possible to be rich without being wise, but you cannot be wise and not end up being rich and successful in your business. When people are rich but lack wisdom, chances are high of them losing their success and never being able to recover. Such men go down in history as foolish men; such was the case of a certain man in the Bible;

'Now there was a man in Maon whose business was in Carmel, and the man was very rich... The name of the man was Nabal.' - 1 Samuel 25:2,3.

Nabal means folly or a fool, yet he was rich! His foolishness helped him take the wrong decisions which eventually cost him his entire fortune. He came to a point in his life when he needed to make a decision; he got it wrong, and to make matters worse, he didn't have any friend, mentor, or counselor he could borrow some wisdom from!

On the other hand, a wise man who falls and loses his business, and all his possessions have the potentials to rise again. A wise man can't be down for long! You know why? Because the wisdom of God at work on him will lift him and show him a new and unforeseen path to wealth!

'That path no bird knows, nor has the falcon's eye seen it. The proud lions have not trodden it, nor has the fierce lion passed over it. He cuts out channels in the rocks, and his eye sees every precious thing. He dams up the streams from trickling; what is hidden he brings forth to light.' – Job 28:7,8,10,11.

God's wisdom is creative and also revelatory. It uncovers secret things and teaches you what you never studied in a college. It gives you strategies on how to get to the top in your business and gives winning ideas! It is wisdom that produces wealth, not blind labor! I pray that you will hear the voice of wisdom everyone it comes to you.

'Receive my instruction and not silver, and knowledge rather than choice gold; For wisdom is better than rubies, and all the things you may desire cannot be compared with her.' - Proverbs 8:10-11.

The economy of your country does not matter to wisdom – you are a new creation in Christ Jesus, and you have been given access to heaven's resources. All the wealth of the entire universe came out of wisdom (See Psalm 104:24). Wisdom has no respect for problems, it will obtain results in any environment, under any circumstances, it will locate hidden treasures out of a dunghill. I encourage you to pursue wisdom with all your being and never give up until you lay your hands on it. Whenever you need to make a decision, find a quiet spot, with your writing materials, pray meditatively, and pull wisdom from God's Spirit!

'O Lord, how manifold are Your works! In wisdom, You have made them all. The earth is full of your riches.' – Psalm 104:24.

Something Extra

Although you have been permitted to prosper by God, there is something you should know. One of the important things to ensure to secure your business as a kingdom business is that it should uniquely meet the needs of people, wealth will simply be a by-product and not the main goal. As you get yourself prepared to be a channel of blessing to others, divine ideas from heaven will flood your heart – and through the wisdom of God – you will be able to interpret them *correctly* and then begin the process of implementing them.

As you have read in the previous section of this book, when we make making money our primary passion or goal, that is a clear sign of the stronghold of mammon in our lives. And as long as we entertain the traits of this evil power – which are greed and covetousness – we might never be able to *fully* access heaven's resources. So, carefully search for an area of your passion that transcends just making money, and when you find it, stay on it, and don't give up.

Did you know that much of King Solomon's wealth came from his fame, and he started getting famous when he met the needs of two confused women who were fighting over a baby? (See 1 Kings 3:16-28). As a matter of fact, in the encounter he had with

God – in which God gave him an open ticket to ask whatever he wanted – we read that he asked for *a wise and understanding heart to judge God's people, that he may discern between good and evil* (See 1 Kings 3:3-13). He didn't ask for gold or silver – his wealth simply came as a by-product of meeting people's needs and solving hard questions (See 1 Kings 10:1-3).

So, here's my final word for you: Make God's dreams your dreams, make His business your business, walk in the guidance of His Spirit and the wisdom of Scriptures, seek out godly and successful mentors and instructors, and never stop believing in yourself! For you have been permitted to PROSPER!

'Beloved, I pray that in every way you may succeed and prosper and be in good health [physically], just as [I know] your soul prospers [spiritually].' – 3rd John 2 AMP.

Made in the USA
Middletown, DE
23 October 2021